Mind
Over
Matter

Halim A. Flowers

ISBN:09 77831825
ISBN-13:9780977831821

Whatsoever man has done, man can do!

(Marcus Garvey)

HALIM A. FLOWERS

CONTENTS

INTRODUCTION

This book is about faith. About believing in yourself, your goals, and having the necessary determination to see it through until you reach your aim. It is about having a direction, staying focused on your desired destination, and persevering all of the hardships that will come along the way. This book is about knowing what you want in life, having the strength to trust your gut instincts to take a risk in pursuit of your success, about overcoming barriers, bouncing back up after getting knocked on the ground, and holding on to firm conviction in your strategy when everyone else has begun to doubt your methods. This book is about challenging yourself to abandon your comfort zone if you have not yet fulfilled what you believe to be your ultimate purpose in life, and going against all human reasoning and logic to obtain that what you always wanted the most, but was too afraid to try because you have always been paralyzed by the fear of failing in your attempt to get it. This book is not about merely striving to just be successful. Rather, this book is about setting out on a path to make history. This book is about accomplishing the impossible. If this book has made it to print, and you are now reading it, then history has already been made on my end. However, this book is not about me, but about you. This book is about destroying the myth that you have to attend the most prestigious universities and get the most degrees to achieve something great in life. This book will show you that most of the people today, and in history, have not left their mark on this world because they went to the best schools or had the richest family. This book will "remind" you that everything you need to begin your journey to accomplishing the impossible is already inside of you. Faith, hope, conviction, determination, trust, patience, and love. Without these things, no college degrees, no riches, and no connections, will help you reach your goals.

Daring To Be Great,

Halim A. Flowers 07-27-09

1 KNOWLEDGE

"Unless you know your destination, there is no way you will be able to chart a course to reach there." (Chika Oyeani)

No one gets into a car without first knowing where *it* is that they want to go; unless a person intends to just joyride. The same principle has to be applied in the ride of our lives. Either you know exactly where you want to go or you just joyride to wherever the vehicle of life takes you.

In order to be successful, you have to know where your success lies at. Once you know where you have to go in order to reach your goals in life, only then can you begin to take the first step on the journey towards your destination.

In order to be successful, you have to know where your success lies at. Once you know where you have to go in order to reach your goals in life, only then can you begin to take the first step on the journey towards your destination.

Most people never get what they really want in life because they have never told themselves what they really wanted. One minute they want this, the next hour they want something completely different. A lot of us are afraid to admit to ourselves that we really do know what we want because we do not know how we are

4

going to get it. This fear of not knowing how we can get what we want paralyzes us to a permanent state of inaction. Therefore, we just joyride in life, not knowing where the journey will take us. We complain about the many dead ends and ditches that life keeps landing us in, and constantly remind others of what they can "never" do.

There is a science to obtaining what you want in life. A science of success. Science derives from the Latin word scientia meaning "having knowledge". This science is no hidden secret. Anyone who has read about the lives of successful people and seriously studied their autobiographies and biographies could clearly detect the underlying principles and spirit that is the common theme in all of their stories. Regardless of ethnicity, religion, location, or time period in history, the science of success has, and continues to, transcend all of the superficial barriers that prevent others from getting what they want in life.

Do you know what you want in life at this moment? If so, then are you ready to dedicate yourself to reaching your goals without wavering to something else by the time you begin reading the next chapter because you do not know how you are going to get to your destination? If you do not know what you want in life right now, then there is no need for you to read any further until you are ready to design your future. Either you know what you want to do with your life or others will know what to do with you!

"When you have nothing to be ashamed of, when you know who you are and what you stand for, you stand in wisdom." Insight, Strength, and Protection: You stand in Peace!

'No weapon formed against you shall prosper.'

Isaiah 54:17

(Oprah Winfrey)

2 VISION

"What we can easily see is a small percentage of what is possible. Imagination is having the vision to see what is just below the surface; to picture that which is essential, but invisible to the eye." (unknown)

You always hear the phrase, "Seeing is believing!" However, most of us, when we hear this famous quote, believe that seeing is something that can only be done with the physical eyes. If only we could realize that we could see more clearly when we close our eyes and be still.

Imagination, the art of forming images in your mind, is the necessary ingredient for cooking up a great plan. If you can see it, you can achieve it. We have all heard that before, but do not understand the full meaning of that statement because we limit our sight to what we can see when our eyes are open.

There once was a man who had an idea to build *a* casino and hotel in a desert. He put so much into his vision that he secured the loan for his investment with his life. The casino and hotel opened in the middle of an empty desert, and not many people came to it. Shortly thereafter, the man with the idea was killed for the failure of his plan. Today, we call that unknown desert where that casino and hotel was built "Las Vegas".

To have vision is to be able to see a casino and hotel where there are only cactus trees and sand. To have vision is to be able to see dry land where there is nothing but muddy water apparent to the naked eye. You have to be able to see the fruits of your plan, your homes, your businesses, your wealth, and your success, before these things ever occur in the physical world. As human beings, where would we be if we relied only on what our eyes could see? Would there be an airplane, an automobile, a computer, a cell phone? The people who invented these things saw them in their minds before they ever made any effort to bring them about outside of their imaginary world inside of them.

The most successful people in this world are those who have the most vivid vision. They do not care about having 20/20 eyesight. They have the gift to sit still, close their eyes, and imagine amazing things that will forever leave an impression upon the world. They can see farther than others, see things happen before others see them, and can see things with their eyes closed that others cannot see with their eyes wide open.

Those with the best vision are able to see things so clearly with their eyes wide shut, that they can convince others to see them with their eyes open. They sell their vision to others!

Most of us will never accomplish anything that we want to do in life because we cannot see how we can do it. If you limit your sight only to what your two eyeballs can see, then your results will always be limited, and you will not have the necessary initiative that is required to be successful. If you cannot see it, then you will not be able to convince yourself or anyone else that you can do anything that they have not seen someone else do before. If they cannot see that it has been done before, then they will never believe that you can do it either.

Do you have a vision of who you want to be and what you want to do in life? Can you not only see it, but can you already feel, touch, taste, smell, and hear it?

3 CONVICTION

"When you have conviction, the impossible loses its inevitability, and you become convinced that you can do what everyone else thinks can never be done."

In order to overcome great obstacles to accomplish great feats in life, you have to be convinced along your journey that you can reach your goals. Conviction is the force that keeps you convicted and imprisoned to all of the people, places, and things that are essential for your success. It is the tool that you will need in order to persuade others to assist you in your endeavors.

A lack of conviction causes you to begin to doubt your own vision. When you are not convinced within yourself about your plan to reach your goals, it will show in your speech and actions, which will clearly demonstrate half-heartedness and a lack of confidence. Not having conviction will prevent you from having the necessary boldness that is required to overcome certain barriers that may appear to be invincible to the common mind.

In life, the majority of people do not have the mind power to overcome the matter. Most people are experts at reminding you of what you can never do. Their lack of conviction to anything denies them the ability to stay focused on doing what they know must be done in their lives. They are afraid to try to do anything outside of the box that their family, peers, and society has set for them because they fear what others will think or say about them if they fail in their efforts. These type of people place more value into the opinions of others who have never accomplished anything worthy of any merit in their own lives, than they value their very own well-being. You need not worry about convincing those who like to remind you of what can never be done. Rather, you only need to assure that you remain convinced that your plan to reach your goals will eventually come through.

Hold on to your conviction. Always reaffirm your conviction by reminding yourself of the reasons that you are convinced that you will be successful. Keep revisiting your strategy in order to strengthen your conviction, and, to make adjustments to your plan that may be needed in order for you to be successful. Remember, the goals stay the same, but the plan to reach the goals can always be changed when needed. Once you possess conviction to your success, you will talk it, eat it, sleep it, dream it, and of all things, walk it.

4 FAITH

"To believe that you will one day obtain what you do not have in your possession at the present moment" That is Faith!

Light, is most appreciated in the darkest of places. And, faith is the light that illuminates the gloomiest moments in our lives. The moments when we feel as though a black cloud is hovering over our heads. The times when we want to just give up and throw in the towel. When it becomes a task just to wake up and find an incentive to get out of bed. Faith is the light that ignites the flame to keep us going forward.

To believe in the unseen, in that what nobody in the world has ever set their sights upon, is not an easy task. Rather, it is an exception to the norm. That is why it is only a few prominent individuals who have found a way to transmit the products of their faith from existing only in their imagination to the world dominated by the limitations of our five senses. Sometimes in life, we have nothing, no one, and no place to seek refuge with. All we have is our faith. Our belief is the only thing that can comfort us. When all odds are stacked against us, it is the light of faith that will raise us against all odds. When everyone tells us to give up and everything informs us that our efforts are in vain, our belief is the driving force that will inspire us to take one more step forward in the direction of our destination. Even though the path is too dark to see where the step will land us.

Faith, like strength, is not known in times of prosperity or ease. What does faith mean to the one who already has everything in their immediate possession? How can one claim to be strong unless one has faced an even stronger opposition?

Faith varies in levels within individuals. Some people have faith as strong as mountains. Others, have faith as flimsy as the house of a spider. Then, most people have no faith at all.

The ultimate faith for most people is in a higher power outside of themselves. And, I gather my strength from that same source as well. However, our Creator who has endowed us all with certain unalienable Rights, that among these are Life, Liberty, and the pursuit of Happiness, manifests His divine power in our individual lives according to the level of Faith that we have in our own minds and hearts in our own abilities to take action to get things done. He only aids and assist us as much as we show Him that we are willing to take the necessary efforts to actualize our belief that He will help us in our journey to reach our goals. Faith is not just an idea in the heart. Belief is also statements of the tongue that are supported by consistent actions.

Do you have faith in yourself? Do you believe that you have what it takes to be successful? Then let your light shine forth in the darkest of moments and places to guide you through gloom.

5 HOPE

"They were not prepared to look optimistically into a future that had to be viewed through a gloomy present."

(Ernesto "Che" Guevara)

Hope and optimism are intertwined by the knit of an inseparable thread. When you are optimistic, you expect the best outcome of any and every situation. Even in the face of tragedy, you are still resilient enough to interpret the calamity as the necessary disaster that was needed to pave the way for your success. That is hope!

Every year you hear about the devastating effects that storms have upon people. When the storm comes, the clouds transform the light of the day into the darkest night. The sun becomes veiled by the eye of the storm. The wind blow violently and converts the most rigid of things like buildings, homes, cars, and boats into flying objects. The waters burst forth into a tidal commotion that floods, drowns, and swallows anything foolish enough to attempt to resist its juggernaut waves.

The storm has always been my favorite similitude to explain the dynamics of hope. When we first set out on our path to accomplish something great in our lives, we cannot see at that moment how we will be successful. The darkness of the clouds of uncertainty is almost enough to compel us to give up before we even attempt to try.

The healing rays and light of the sun abandons us when all of those who we thought would be our best supporters turn

out to be our biggest critics. Even our own
loved ones express nothing but pessimism
towards our goals and plans to be successful. It
is at this moment that the winds began to blow
the hardest and sweeps us off of our feet.

As the storm throws us in any
direction it desires, we look for a safe place to
land. Our only refuge is our vision, conviction,
and faith in our ability to reach our goals. When
we finally land safely, then the rain decides to
pour all of its reserves upon us. Wet, cold, and
treading against the tidal waves of people's
defeatism forecast and our own despair of our
pitiful present condition, we feel as though the
weight of the world is upon our shoulders.

It is at this point here, at the lowest of the low, that the distinction is made between the common and the great. The average will put their tail between their legs and take shelter in the first source of refuge that will comfort them and say, "I told you so!" In contrast, the exceptional individual will keep fighting against the waves until the tide is conquered to a state of calmness at his feet. He will look directly at the eye of the storm, and without words, declare that he will remain firmly grounded upon his path and will not be shaken by its winds. And the storm will calm.

After this, the one who will reach the unreachable will look at the darkness of the sky. And, where everyone else sees gloom, all he can vision is that there is an ever-present sun always shining behind the superficial clouds. Then the sky turns bright. Still unsatisfied, this defiant individual refuses to claim victory and stop resisting until the heavens binds to his will power and offer a gift of a rainbow for all of the troubles that it took him through along his path. He smiles, while preparing for the next annual storm.

It is our hope that will give us the strength to persevere the afflictions that the storms of life will send our way. The storms are life's cynical way of demonstrating to us how much we really want to reach our goals. To show us what we are willing to sacrifice to be successful. When the winds blow the hardest and every direction we look shows us nothing but infinite darkness, it is our hope that can still vision and feel the healing powers of the sun's rays. Our hope intoxicates our senses to see the illusion of the rainbow in the reality of the hurricane.

Are you ready to have hope in yourself and your plans to be successful? Are you prepared for the storms that life will send your way? Will the storm increase your hope or your despair? Will you tuck and run or stand and tread forward against the winds and tide?

6 INSTINCT

Instinct – A largely inheritable and unalterable tendency of an organism to make a complex and specific response to environmental stimuli without involving reason.

(Franklin E- Dictionary)

There are times while on your road to success, you will be forced to make a spontaneous critical decision. This decision will either propel you towards your goals swiftly or set you back years in your quest. This choice will have to be made rapidly without you being afforded the chance to consult with anyone or any source of information. This crucial next move will only be able to be influenced by the voice from within.

Your instinct, your ability to be able to listen to and understand the feeling in your gut, is a vital weapon in the path to success. You have to be in tune with your inner self to be able to hear what your intuition is attempting to inform you. This is a gift that cannot be taught in any learning institution or completely explained in any book. This is a natural phenomenon that has to be actualized through experiences and developed over time.

How many times have you gone against your gut instinct? How many times have everything inside of you commanded you to do or not do something and you went against the impulse of your intuition? How many times have you suffered for going against the force within you?

A lot of things in our culture serves to destroy our ability to listen to our instinct. If we are not talking, we are watching television, or listening to music, or eating and drinking. Either we are working or worrying about how the next check will not cover all of our expenses. Very rarely do we set aside any time in our lives to sit still and listen to what our inner self has to teach us. We have placed so much emphasis on formal institutional learning, that if every genetic fiber in our bodies tried to persuade us to embark upon a course, and yet "book knowledge" and traditional doctrines taught us to do otherwise, most of us would deny the instruction of our own souls in that specific situation for the general advice of someone else who has never experienced our unique predicament. We conform instead of improvising.

Relying too much on traditional thinking cripples the development of the instinctive intelligence muscle. Like all muscles, the intuition muscle can only grow as strong as the power of its opposition. The more you concentrate on it and try to understand its language in the most dire of situations, the more it will learn to trust that you are willing to listen to its instruction, and the more willing it will be to grant you the gift of its priceless wisdom that was divinely engrained in the core of your existence. The "gut" instinct!

7 DETERMINATION

"When you follow your instincts with firm resolution and resilient tenacity, then doors will begin to open for you where there were once only walls."

Your determination will only be as strong as the intensity to which you have become convinced that the path you are taking will guarantee your success. When you have reached this firm resolve inside your mind, your speech, your ears, your eyes, the hands that you touch with, the feet that you walk with, will all submit to the invincibility of your plan to reach your goals. Every fiber of your existence will begin to be in tune with your desired destination to the point where you will have the habit of experiencing what people like to identify as "good luck".

When you are determined that your strategy is as good as gold, and that you are willing to sacrifice every unnecessary pleasure, pastime, and idle moments of waste in order to be successful, you will initiate a continuous chain of phenomena in your life which will habitually bring you closer to your destination. These occurrences are what we like to describe as "coincidence".

There is no such thing as luck, or coincidence. When preparation meets opportunity, this is what others call luck. When you have thought, spoken, fine-tuned your ears to hear and your eyes to see success, when you have ate, drank, tasted, dreamed, and felt it, then it is not by chance that your life seems to always bring you into contact and harmony with the people, places, and things that help further your progression towards success. This is not luck or coincidence. This is the magnetic force of the power of your concentrated and focused thoughts and ideas in your mind bending matter to assist you with reaching your destination, your destiny.

I often tell people that there is no greater magnetic attraction on this planet than the most frequent thoughts inside of a person's mind and heart. These thoughts are reinforced by emotions, energy in motion, like love, fear, anger, and vengeance. The more passionate you are about something, the more energy you are able to put into motion to pull that thing in your direction. Fear, anger, and vengeance are toxic emotions that eventually destroy the mind and heart from its natural balance, but even they are often utilized to aid an individual with reaching their aim. You have to be passionate about your dreams, your ambitions, and your plans to acquire them. The more passionate you are, the more energy you will have at your disposal to magnetically attract everything you need towards you that is required to secure your success. When you are determined to reach your goals and can formulate an intimate relationship with your blueprint for success, you will be able to express your faith in yourself with a passionate charisma that will even bend the hearts of your enemies into your grace and favor.

Have you made the determination in your mind to be successful? Do you have the tenacity to never say die? Are you capable of maintaining the resilience to never quit your journey no matter what attempts to oppose your progression? If failure is no longer an option for you, then how can you ever fail?

8 TRUST

"Trust is a mental, emotional, spiritual, financial, and physical security deposited and expected to be fulfilled."

In life, you get what you put out. You receive what your hands have earned. You reap what you sow. This has become a universal principle accepted as an uncontestable truth. However, when the reaping does not come when people expect it to harvest, then they begin to question what they once accepted as an absolute truth.

You have to remember that all your actions first take place in the realm of your mind. Your thoughts dictate your speech and the movements of your body limbs. Therefore, if you want to reap big rewards, you must first begin to think great thoughts. I like to call this "Power Thinking".

A lot of times people tell you that the sky is the limit. In contrast, I tell you to reach beyond the limits of the sky. In the world outside of this planet is what is known as infinite "space", so do not limit your ideas to what is finite. Think big!

If you have planted good seeds, removed the weeds of pessimistic people and negative places and things that will stunt the growth of your flowers from blossoming, and watered your crop, then as long as the light of the sun shines upon your soil, your harvest is sure to come. You have to trust the process of your sowing. You have to trust that you will reap.

Life is seasonal. Likewise, so is harvesting. It is not always fall and winter, nor will it always be the good weather of the spring and summer. Everything has its due place and time in life. If you are sowing good seeds, then you have to trust that the harvest is on its way. Yet in still, you cannot part with the reality that harvesting is not something that occurs all year around. You have to experience the harshness of the cold dead winter.

You have to be secure within your mind that your soils, your plans to reach your goals, are fertile. That your field will produce the fruits of your labor. Even when the results that you anticipate do not happen the exact moment that you planned them to, that you must be secure that your harvest is destined to come. You have to trust your destiny.

A lot of people are quick to say that they trust their God, but some of them are not secure with themselves. They utilize their belief in their Creator as a shield for their low self-esteem and lack of drive to take the initiative to commit themselves to pursuing what they want in life. David did not defeat Goliath by trusting in his God alone without any actions to substantiate his belief. He threw the small stone with the trust that his God would assist his effort to take down a big opponent. He was secure with himself enough to have the courage to even think about throwing the stone.

Do you believe that you will reap what you sow? Do you trust that the soils of your plans to reach your goals are fertile to bear the fruits of your success? If so, trust in your ability to sow the seeds, and anticipate your

9 PATIENCE

"Where there is hardships, afflictions, and desires awaiting to be fulfilled, there you will find patience."

There are three aspects of patience. The patience of adhering to what is morally right, the patience of abstaining from what is morally wrong, and the patience with enduring destiny and fate. The rewards for patience are great. However, patience is a virtue that escapes most of humanity. It is not patience for you to do the right thing in times of prosperity. Your patience is tested when it is more convenient for you to do what you know to be wrong and harmful instead of enduring the hardships that will come along with doing what you know to be the right thing to do. We live in a society of convenience that caters to the instant gratification of our wants and needs. Therefore, when it becomes easier and faster for us to receive what we desire by doing what is wrong, we choose to do it, regardless of the long term consequences. Hence the high rate of debt that individuals and our country continues to find themselves in. The immediate gain at the peril of the near future. No patience!

Patience with the calamities that descend upon your destiny is defined by your initial response taken when the crisis first occurs in your life. When you lose control of yourself at the first sight of adversity, then you lose claim to the virtue of patience. No matter how much control you may gain over yourself the next hour, next day, next week, next month or year, your lack of control over yourself when immediately reacting to your affliction dictates whether you were patient or not. Your patience will be deferred to your next initial response to a hardship.

It is the trials and tribulations that inform yourself and the world around you how much you are willing to sacrifice and endure to succeed. The obstacles along your journey to impede your progress are necessary to test and develop your mental prowess and will power to endure the storms that are required to clear the path of the road that leads to your achievements. It is your level of patience that will determine your resilience to continue planting the seeds in your soil when the fruits of the harvest have yet to begin to sprout at a time where you had expected them to already have been alive, ripe, and eaten.

Where there is no adversity or desires unfulfilled, there can be no patience. Where there is no patience, there can be no resolve nor strength to overcome resistance and opposition. It is hardships that mold the mettle of men, and how they respond to unexpected crisis situations defines their level of mental muscle. Patience is the strength enhancer for the power of the mind. With small tests, come tiny rewards. With great crisis confronted with an even more intense level of patience, a mind can begin to move great things like mountains and the hearts of nations.

Hardships in life are guaranteed to meet your destiny. There is no path except that it will have its bumps and barriers. What will be your initial response to adversities?

10 LOVE

"It is ▪the combination of thought and love which forms the irresistible forced of the law of attraction." (Charles Haanel)

The love of a mother zebra for the safety of offspring will compel her to resist the attack of a pride of starving lioness. The desire of a man to win a residence of love within the heart of a woman he cherishes will inspire him to do things that he never imagined he would ever be capable of doing. Love lends wings!

Just because you may have goals, and plans to reach them, does not necessitate that you love the process of what you are doing to fulfill your vision. When you reach the point in your quest where you are disappointed at night with the setting of the sun because the nature of your body has compelled you to a sleep that separates you from your task, when you dream vividly of your success, and when the rising of the sun in the morning completely overwhelms all of your senses with excitement because you were anxious to awaken to continue your efforts towards your success, then you know for sure at that moment that you are intimately involved with your plans to achieve your goals. When you are in love with what you are doing, you cannot be easily distracted nor persuaded away from your purpose.

People tend to be amazed by the achievements of successful individuals. They wonder how Kobe Bryant can invest five hours daily practicing his shot, how Beyoncé can annually maintain a high quality of entertainment expressions, how a paraplegic like Stephen Hawkins can be the leading scientist of astrophysics, and the audacity of Barack Obama to hope to be President of the United States of America. It is the love for what they all do that is the underlying sentiment that inspires them to excel at what they do. Love is the key!

In life, you will encounter many things that will motivate you to take actions towards obtaining your goals. However, you will find no greater force on this earth to inspire you to succeed than the emotion of love. When you can grow to love what you are doing to reach your success, and the person that your efforts are transforming you into, then it is only a matter of time before you will attract all of the people, places, and things that will facilitate you accomplishing the impossible.

Do you seriously love everything about what you are doing in order to be successful? Have you developed an intimate relationship and passionate emotional attachment with the person you are developing into along your path to achieve your goals? Can you live without the love of reaching for your ultimate success? If so, then this book was not for you. Do not love the one you can live with, love the one that you cannot live without!

AFTERWORD

"Most of us sooner or later, find that, at critical points in our lives, we must strike out on our own to make a path where none exists." (Elaine Pagels)

This book is dedicated to all of those who say, "Never"! This book is for everyone who has forfeited their dreams because they were too afraid to fail. Those who never knew that the only failure was the choice to never reach for what they always wanted.

After writing and reading this book chapter for chapter, there is not much more that I can say but that *I* take absolutely no credit for what it contains except for the errors within it. It only took me two weeks to finish this book; therefore, I know that this is divinely inspired. It is bigger than me.

The only thing that I would like to add is that if you really believe in what this book entails, and then begin to apply it immediately in your life. I can promise you from my own personal experiences that what is impossible will start to bend your way. At first you will be shocked and may say; "This is crazy!", in amazement with how things will begin to fall in your lap effortlessly at times. Just remember that love and thoughts generate an irresistible energetic force within you that will magnetically attract your success towards you. Lose your shock factor and expect the best and beyond!

My good friend Neil Hilliard likes to remind me that people are looking for road maps to find their destination, but I am a person who makes my own road maps. Therefore, I encourage you to not wait for others to dictate what path you should follow to get to your destination, your destiny. Make your own roadmap!

Don't be afraid to travel down a path that your gut instinct tells you to follow, even though the world may say that it is a dead end. Make a road where none exists! Trust your destiny!

In Pursuit of The Impossible,

Halim A. Flowers
08-10-09

(P.S.) I did it my way!

www.ingramcontent.com/pod-product-compliance
Lightning Source LLC
Chambersburg PA
CBHW060053050426

42448CB00011B/2433